THE HOME-BASED BUSINESS GUIDE TO

WRITE-OFF

ALMOST ANYTHING!

THE HOME-BASED BUSINESS GUIDE TO

WRITE-OFF

ALMOST ANYTHING!

You'll Keep More Money Once You Know
These Tax Secrets

DOUG COLLINS

The author does not dispense tax advice, but only offers information of a general nature to help you in your quest for personal and business financial success. This book is not designed to be a definitive tax guide or to take the advice of a qualified tax professional who is familiar with home-based tax write-offs in your state, province, or country. In the event you use the information in this book for yourself, the author assumes no responsibility for your actions.

Published August 6, 2020 by Doug Collins

Cataloguing in Publication is on file with the Library and Archives Canada and the Library of Congress Control Number: 2020917202

Paperback ISBN: 978-1-7772952-0-2

For information about purchasing bulk copies of this book at a discount, you can reach the author at doug.collins@mail.com or at DougCollinsOnline.com.

"More than 9 in 10 business owners were overpaying on their taxes – regardless of whether they were paying for a high-priced accountant or not. Too many tax advisors just don't know or care about all the opportunities in the tax rules, and their clients can pay dearly because of it. What does that mean to you? It means if you own a business, there's a 93% chance you are bleeding needless family wealth by paying way too much tax."

- Forbes Magazine

CONTENTS

FOREWORD

Doug Collins and I met over a decade ago. He was introduced to me "as a someone I needed to know". Doug is located on the east coast of Canada. The Maritimes are historically a market believed to be difficult to penetrate when businesses are seeking to expand. Our mutual contact believed Doug might be the right contact for me.

Doug and I immediately connected, and I instantly understood how truly gifted he was. At the time Doug was a respected marketing executive for an international supplier in Canada, and he seemed to grasp the opportunity I was offering him. It did not take him long to completely understand the potential he was reviewing and so began our long-term friendship and business relationship.

Shortly after our introduction, Doug became aware of the fact that he was going to be caught in the middle of a massive merger which would likely result in him either having to choose to relocate to a different area of Canada or get the 'unceremonious downsize' complete with a severance package.

Needless to say, he took the package and remained in the area he loved to live for so many reasons. However, it opened the door for him to finally fulfill his long-held dream to become self-employed and work from home.

As he embraced this long-held vision, working from home, he found some serious shortfalls in information and guidance for committed home-based entrepreneurs. He also found some big prejudices from tax preparers and bookkeepers who service these folks. He realized, if he had to rely on the tax preparer he was using to do a truly accurate and professional service for him, he would need to become more well versed in the skill of record and account keeping.

He also discovered these tax preparers were not going to proactively look for his legitimate tax write-offs and if he was not well prepared each year, he was going to be giving the government money that was rightfully his.

Doug also came to understand he was not alone in this complaint. Everywhere he looked people had the same challenges. Tax preparers were urging and recommending small businesses curtail their expensing of legitimate tax write-offs. Tax preparers were suggesting these business folks could not claim the tax write-offs they were legitimately entitled to, resulting in individuals failing to claim what was truly their right, for fear of the 'Taxman' and being audited. Yet, if you asked someone at the CRA or IRS they would tell you 'if you do not claim it, you won't get it!'

In reading this book, you will discover, this is as an introduction to how to keep more of your money through legitimate tax write-offs. This indicates to me you are either already in a home-based business or you are thinking about one and trying to evaluate if you having a home-based business might be worth the effort.

The answer from my perspective is a resounding YES, either part-time or full-time, and the tax write-offs you create can make the difference in your financial status in so many ways that I cannot even begin to emphasize this to you effectively.

If you have received this book as a gift or purchased it out of curiosity, allow me to direct you to your Next Step...

This is where your journey begins. The next step is to, Go the Distance, allow yourself to become truly skilled in this part of your home business. You will be glad you did!

Darlene Long, *28 Year Veteran in Home Business and Recipient of the* Direct Sellers Association (DSA Canada) *2017 Mark of Distinction Award*

PREFACE

WHO THIS BOOK IS FOR (AND WHAT IT IS NOT ABOUT)!

Hey, my name is Doug Collins. Before we get started, I wanted to let you know who this book is for and more importantly, what this book is not about.

This book is NOT a "how to" file income tax returns. Its purpose is to empower you to be proactive with your tax write-offs, to be fully prepared for tax season, and maybe even enjoy tax season because you know you will be keeping more money for yourself.

This book is for all those sole proprietors who have the courage to venture into their home-based business, operating from home with no physical store location such as: freelancers, contractors, coaches, course creators, affiliate marketers, direct sales and network marketers, real estate investors, as well as the app-based transportation and food delivery drivers, and other gig economy workers.

This book is also to encourage others to consider the benefits of starting home-based business as a tax strategy, as well as for all the other benefits.

This book will take you on a journey to find more tax write-offs and pay less income tax, so that you keep more of your hard-earned money. You don't need to be a tax expert to know what you can write-off in a home-based business. This book will be another important piece in your entrepreneurial journey, one that is often overlooked, largely ignored, and mostly misunderstood. That is what this book is about.

INTRODUCTION

I was inspired to write this book at a time when we were all on a lockdown in our homes because of the pandemic of 2020. As I watched the US and Canadian governments handout billions of dollars, I wondered how this money would ever be paid back. In the years and decades to come, I envisioned the governments fabricating new ideas and creative schemes to increase taxes to support the massive growing debt load.

As I continued to write this book, stories begin to appear in the media, like *"Prepare for a CRA Tax Hike"* written by Brian Paradza of The Motley Fool Canada on June 26, 2020, and was widely reported in the news across Canada. I knew I had to finish this book and get this information into your hands. That media story went on to say:

"Canadians are arguably the highest-taxed citizens of North America today. However, the Canada Revenue Agency (CRA) could still hike tax rates in the near future so as to cover the deep deficits created by economic stimulus packages and household income support programs during the COVID-19 pandemic."

My biggest challenge, when I decided to take on writing this book was figuring out how to keep these ideas simple and generic enough for the home-based business, specifically applicable anywhere in North America, yet detailed and informative enough to allow you, the reader, to have a transformation that will change your tax-paying future forever. After all, how do you teach taxation concepts to an entrepreneur and keep it interesting?

Some of you might be shocked that nowhere in this book will you see a reference to tax forms or tax codes related to any specific government. I didn't reference specific tax forms in this book because I wanted this to remain generic for you. This is not a book about filing your income taxes. Instead, I will be focusing on strategies that don't change, including:

1. How to find more legitimate home-based deductions.
2. How to understand all the business deductions you can take.
3. Speak intelligently with your tax preparer, if you decide to use one.
4. Significantly reduce your chances of being audited.
5. Legally put more money back in your pocket.
6. Become bullet-proof in your record keeping.

It is my goal here to help you avoid mistakes or omissions, and overcome any bad advice you may have received, and allow you to start claiming the tax savings you deserve. In the chapters that follow I'm going to give you a foundation of knowledge, answer some of the most commonly asked questions, take you through the many tax strategies you can use to save thousands on your taxes, and make yourself audit-proof through your record keeping.

In Section One, you will learn that, as a home-based business, it is your responsibility to understand what you can and cannot write-off, and to keep it organized for tax purposes. We will also discuss some of the most common questions and complaints I have heard from others in this home-based business space.

In Section Two, I will go into more detail on the home-based write-offs for which we are eligible. I will offer some tips and strategies to maximize these write-offs while remaining perfectly within the taxation laws.

Finally, Section Three will reveal how to record and calculate these tax write-offs. I think you might be surprised where and how you can save thousands of dollars every year by diverting a percentage of your monthly household living expenses you are already spending into a home-based business tax write-off.

My goal in this book is to simplify what I once believed was a complicated mystery that stressed me out. I'm going to help you see how easy it really is to understand.

This book is for you if you operate any kind of business from home or are considering the benefits of operating a business from home. The information in these pages, when followed, will be worth thousands of dollars in tax savings each year!

This book will teach you:

- Why everyone should have a home-based business.
- Why write-offs bring the greatest tax savings.
- How to increase your home-based business profitably without increasing sales.
- Why people with a home-based business are unknowingly giving away thousands to the government every year.
- How to write-off more personal expenses, including dinners, entertainment, and vacations.
- How to ensure you are audit-proof.

I've spent over two decades learning these concepts and applying these home-based tax strategies. I'm excited to give them to you here now.

Every year, millions of home-based businesses start and stop because 'would-be entrepreneurs' don't have the essential skills including sales and marketing. There's one skill that if learned, I believe they'd never give-up on their home-based business. That's tax write-offs and the benefits it offers. This is what I get excited about and so should you. It's a tragedy that most never learn about this.

Every year during tax season millions of home-based business owners gather their receipts in preparation for filing their taxes. They feel a sense of anxiety handing it over to their tax preparer, and then they cross their fingers they don't owe more in income tax. Does this sound familiar?

For all those who fall into this each year, it's a tragedy as you are missing out on thousands of dollars in tax savings that you could keep in your bank accounts. What nobody is telling you is that handing over that bag of receipts to your tax preparer is not an effective tax strategy.

I know the subject of Income Tax is not the most glamorous of topics. But I love it...!!! It is a necessary and important part of having a home-based business, and in life. The government says it's mandatory to file income taxes.

I want to start our journey here with some of the fundamentals of having a home business from a tax perspective, including a few topics and strategies that took me the last decade to figure out. I call home-based business tax write-offs a secret because after decades of helping others, it became obvious that so many home-based business owners are not aware of this information, and it is costing them!

I first started in my home-based business on a part-time basis back in 1998. At that time, I was like everyone else, bringing my bag of receipts to my tax preparer at tax season, expecting him to do his magic on my income tax. For many years I had little knowledge about preparing and filing taxes. In fact, I was like everyone else; taxes and dealing with a tax preparer stressed me out so much I didn't really want anything to do with it.

Since 2009, I have made it my mission to learn all there is to know about home-based business taxes and claiming tax write-offs. There are just so many legitimate and legal home-based tax strategies that are not generally discussed, even among tax preparers. It really does appear to be a secret.

When it comes to operating a business from home, there's one single important ingredient that most are missing, and that is understanding what you can and cannot write-off on your taxes, as a result of having a home-based business. Having this knowledge and confidence can be one of your greatest financial breakthroughs.

If you're already in a business, get ready, buckle up, and let's go. If you're interested in starting your own home business, you're going to see how simple this is and how simple it can be to leverage these tax savings. So, let's get going.

Knowledge Is Power

CHAPTER 1

Tax Benefits of a Home-Based Business

The home-based businesses trend is quickly becoming the fastest growing form of business start-up. In an article written by Jason Azar in Forbes on Sep 9, 2013, it was stated that *"52% of all small businesses are home-based"*. Starting a business from home is much easier today with the internet, low cost of entry, simplified technology, and social media. It allows flexibility, especially with a part-time effort, in comparison to starting a traditional small business outside the home.

Working from home in a home-based business requires self-discipline, but the benefits can be substantial especially for tax purposes, with the greatest tax advantages in the start-up years.

Many of us have interesting stories that led us to decide to start a home-based business, and what drives us to continue every day bringing value to others. My own personal experience with these tax write-offs has been a strong motivation for me to help others through the message in this book.

I have been through a number of government tax audits and reassessments over the last decade. I know the importance of being organized and having good record keeping. Who remembers any level of detail going back 2, 3, or 4 years? It always comes down to well organized and accurate documentation to support your claims.

In 2015, I was reassessed by Revenue Canada and received a letter advising me of their decision that included a bill for over $15,000 they claimed I now owed for back taxes plus interest and penalty charges. This reassessment spanned over the previous three years. I knew they were wrong in this assessment, so I wrote an objection letter. A response came back months later with their decision that my objection was denied and I owed this money. I then wrote another objection letter, this time adding more details and an explanation of the points where they had made their mistakes. Again, months later the second objection was denied.

I then contacted a former Revenue Canada Tax Collector who is now a freelance consultant specializing in these kinds of complicated situations. After reviewing my situation, he said I had almost a zero chance of winning this dispute with the government. By this time, I had now filed two objection letters, and it was almost a year later. He advised me that if I sent him a $1,700 retainer, he would help me file a third objection letter. He said Revenue Canada almost never reverses their decisions after two objection letters. But I could always try again.

I was not going to give up! I knew I was right. I knew I had the record keeping to prove my case. I just needed to present it to them so they could see my side of it. Not an easy task, but I was not going to back down. I decided that nobody knows my situation and record keeping better than I, so I spent days preparing that third objection letter.

This time my response came with copies of supporting documents and receipts going point-by-point in detail over the previous three years. I included print outs of Facebook posts as evidence of time, location and purpose; copies of plane tickets, bank statements, expense receipts, home expense bills and more covering the previous three years. I attached a very detailed four-page letter that reference each attachment, it read like a legal affidavit being filed in court. I shipped the documents off to the tax department in a box and set it aside. Six months later I received a letter in the mail advising me of their final decision that they sided with me and my balance was being cancelled. I won!

The lesson here is that there are no hard and fast rules when it comes to claiming tax write-offs. There are some clearly defined guidelines and other areas that are open to interpretation. When it comes to tax write-offs, if we feel it is justified (and legal) we have to make sure we always have documentation to support it.

In the end it was my record keeping and very detailed response combined with my persistence to stand up for myself that won that tax battle. On two other occasions I received letters from Revenue Canada as a "random verification audit" and both times I sent them an over-the-top very detailed response and never heard back.

There have books written on the benefits of having a home-based business but few that really go into these benefits from a tax write-off standpoint. This book is written by a home-based entrepreneur for the home-based entrepreneur. Knowing what you can and cannot write-off on your taxes is the difference between keeping thousands in your pocket each year, and giving it to the government.

As we go through this Section One, we will tackle some of the most commonly asked questions and misunderstandings there are when it comes to home-based business tax write-offs. I am bringing this book to you from a home-based business owner perspective with the objective to empower you to have the knowledge, confidence, and skills to maximize your tax write-offs, thereby saving you thousands annually starting this year.

The most popular form of home-based business is the Sole Proprietorship. A sole proprietorship is a business with a single owner, most often no employees and is not registered as a corporation or limited liability company (LLC). One of the more common forms of sole proprietor whom I work with most often is an independent distributor who represents a direct sales or network marketing company. There are other types of home-based businesses who operate from their home with no physical store location such as; freelancers, contractors, gig economy workers, coaches, affiliate marketers, as well as all the app-based transportation and food delivery drivers and other gig economy workers who can fall into this category as well.

The moment you start offering any type of goods and services to others, the government automatically considers you to be a sole proprietorship. It's really that simple. As a sole proprietor, from the government's standpoint, there is no distinction between you and your business. It is not necessary to create a separate business or trade name; many sole proprietors do business under their own names.

As a sole proprietorship business, you are entitled to all profits and are responsible for all your business losses, liabilities, and taxes on your income. The biggest difference between doing your income taxes as a sole proprietor and doing them just as an employee is that you have to report your business's "profits and losses" on an extra form.

This is where the interesting part comes in, as we will begin to look at the amazing opportunity from a tax write-off standpoint. As a home-based sole proprietor, you report your business income and expenses on your personal income tax. This would also include your full-time income if you are employed. I believe every person should have a home-based business, and every traditional small business owner should consider the benefits of having a home-based office for their business.

A traditional business or franchise, depending on what type you decide to start, could cost anywhere from tens of thousands of dollars to hundreds of thousands of dollars or even millions. In 2011, I opened a traditional bricks and mortar business with an initial investment of $80,000, and much more for expansion throughout the three years it was in operation. The business received plenty media publicity and recognition in the community; however, I made a lifestyle decision to close the doors and liquidate the assets as my time was better invested in focusing on my home-based business.

I'm not against a traditional business, however not everyone is in a position of having to leverage that amount of start-up capital when the odds are stacked against it from surviving in 3 to 5 years. This is exactly why I am so passionate about home-based business, and advocate considering partnering up with a direct sales or network marketing company. The start-up costs in these opportunities are reasonably priced and allow you to begin on a part-time basis, with all the upside of the home-based tax write-offs.

It's important to note that you can't just sign up with a direct sales company and expect tax deductions. You have to attempt to earn an income. We will get more into it later in the book.

It has been widely reported that Canada and the US pay more in taxes than in food, housing, transportation, and clothing combined. Having a home-based business allows you to redirect many of these every day living expenses into legitimate home-based tax write-offs. Lowering your taxes is one of the quickest ways to put cash back in your pocket.

In the chapters that follow, I am going to show you why starting a home-based business will allow you to never overpay taxes to the government again. But first, lets take a look at what defines a home-based business from the government's perspective.

CHAPTER 2

Definition of "Home-Based Business"

The definition of a business is 'an activity that you conduct for profit or with a reasonable expectation of making a profit'. As we discussed in the previous chapter, any time you begin to offer for sale a product or service, you are a sole proprietor; you are in business.

When it comes to the government and determining if you are eligible for tax write-offs, they are likely to apply what is called the "profit test". The profit test refers to the business definition used by the government and is used to determine whether or not a person who claims to be operating a business really is, or is it a hobby activity. The government will generally not allow expenses to be claimed for hobbies.

If a person claims to be operating a home-based business and he/she does not pass the profit test, all of the claimed business write-offs would be disallowed - creating a hefty tax bill.

The profit test simply asks, "Was the activity conducted with an actual expectation to earn a profit?" and "Was that expectation of profit reasonable?". For example, here are some of the criteria the government would use to determine the reasonable expectation of profit for a home-based business activity by an individual:

❏ The profit and loss experience in past years
❏ The amount of gross income, if any, reported over several years
❏ The length of time over which a profit could reasonably be expected to be shown must be relevant to the nature of the activity
❏ The extent of activity in relation to that of a business of a comparable nature and size in the same industry
❏ The amount of time spent on the business activity in question
❏ The individual's qualifications, such as experience, training, and education
❏ The capability of the home business to show a profit sometime in the future
❏ The evidence of efforts in promoting the products or services with the intent to make a profit
❏ The type of expenses claimed and their reasonableness to the ability to create a profit
❏ The nature of the product or service supplied, such that it has a profit potential by filling a void or need in the marketplace

While some of these criteria might be subjective in nature, it always comes back to the record keeping of your business activities and claiming reasonable expenses for the size and type of home business you have.

This does not change the fact that you can claim tax write-offs, but it does say that it's important to know the rules and have a good grasp on what you can and cannot legitimately write-off for your home-based business.

My goal for writing this book is to empower the home-based business owner to be a business within the government definition, and to ensure they are taking every tax write-off available, and have solid record keeping that allows them to be audit-proof.

CHAPTER 3

Tax Season is Designed to Pay More Income Tax

When I started my first home-based business in 1998, I would put receipts and paperwork in a folder marked "business". Then tax season arrived; that was when the overwhelming and intimidating experience all began.

Back in those days, I did not know exactly what I was doing when it came to taxes or what specifically I could write-off in my part-time home-based business, but I did get some tax relief on my employment income. I was using a tax preparer at that time who completed tax returns for other home-based businesses. I always figured he knew what he was doing.

Things went along like this for many years, generally being disorganized and leaving it up to that tax preparer to handle it for me each tax season.

This is me in August 1998, in my early years having a home-based business. Computers back in those days cost about $5,000, that's approximately $7,400 in today's value. I recall the company I worked for at the time had supported the staff in putting together an employee purchase plan for personal computers at home. So, a payment plan was a great way to get technology at home, and my goal was to take my home-based business online. My tax preparer never told me I could write-off any of that monthly payment as part of a home-based business expense.

Over the years I learned more about tax write-offs and collected more expense receipts that I could claim on my taxes. But it wasn't until the 2009 tax season when everything changed. That's when I started a new part-time home-based business in the network marketing profession while working full-time in my corporate career. Now with a decade of experience, combined with more knowledge and confidence, that year I received a $6,600 tax refund when I was expecting to owe $5,000 as I did the previous year. That worked out to be an $11,600 difference on my taxes simply from claiming these home-based tax write-offs from my new start-up business.

That's when I knew I was on to something, but I knew I was still missing more receipts and I questioned what potential tax write-offs was I not aware of. These questions started me on a journey of learning tax-related information that transformed everything.

I soon started to see that tax season was designed to work against us. When we step back and think about it, we can see it. We go through the year not thinking much about taxes until tax season. But by then we are already into another year, and we are left looking back at the previous year. Who ever remembers what we did all last year in any great detail? Preparing income taxes is a snap-shot of the year captured from receipts we hand over to a tax preparer. But even for the tax preparer, tax season is their busiest time of the year. They're working long hours over a very short period of time, often just 8 to 10 weeks, to service all of their clients. Other than that, for the most part, nobody thinks about it the other ten months of the year.

We work all year long earning an income; we pay our taxes, and then it's tax season. Most tax preparers do not have the time to sit with you and analyze the details of your tax return, make recommendations to capture more expenses on that return or the coming years. In many cases, from the complaints I hear often, many tax preparers do not even understand home-based business, especially those who are in a direct sales or network marketing type of business, and more often discourage their clients from filing their income taxes as a business.

21

In the next few chapters, you will learn what the majority of home-based business owners don't understand, the bad advice they are getting from tax preparers, and what you need to know to not only be successful in business but also how to save thousands of dollars of income tax every year.

The first step is to look at the tax write-offs you are not currently claiming and are slipping through the cracks. Your tax preparer may not be looking for them and may not be as committed to your income and home-based business as you are. Most tax preparers are conservative by nature and are focused on reporting taxes based on what you provided to them, what they know about home-based business, and how they interpret the tax code.

As taxpayers, we are all responsible to know what we can claim and how far we can legally increase tax write-offs to reduce our income tax obligations. If you're taking your receipts to your tax preparer and expecting him/her to find every possible opportunity for write-offs, you are already too late. These should have been proactively taken and recorded correctly throughout the year, and I'm going to help you change and be more focused on tax planning.

CHAPTER 4

Your Tax Preparer is Giving You Bad Advice

I have encountered so many instances where a tax preparer has given extremely bad advice to those with a home-based business, especially those who have a part-time business.

A few years ago, I had someone contact me who had enrolled in a home-based direct sales business. This person had such a great personal experience with the company, they decided to become a distributor to share it with others and build a part-time home-based business alongside their full-time job. They were disappointed when they went to their tax preparer to file their income tax as a sole proprietor and was told it was not a legitimate business. They were discouraged from considering going this way on their taxes. This seems to be one of the more common reasons why many who have a home-based business experience the feelings of anxiety and stress when it comes to dealing with their tax preparer.

Unfortunately, there are so many who face this challenge with their tax preparers. Having a home-based business is a great tax strategy, but it is not a lottery ticket. The truth is, that bag of unsorted crinkled up receipts does make a home-based business and is not in your best financial interest for tax purposes. It is not me who knows this to be true, here is a comment I received from a tax preparer who is a member of my Home Business Tax Secrets Facebook Group:

"As a bookkeeper, this is good advice. I get sent plastic bags of crumpled receipts, unopened bills and bank statements, etc. If you organize your papers, you won't have to pay someone like me $50+/hour to sort and uncrumple your receipts and open your mail, before I can even add up your receipts."

I believe the reason so many tax preparers discourage people from claiming home-based business write-offs is the low profit, the lack of record keeping and evidence to show "intent to make a profit", and their lack of understanding about home-based business in general. For some, the business often appears to be a hobby. We will get into this more in Chapter 7.

This is why it's so important as a home-based business to have the knowledge of what you can write-off for tax purposes. It does not matter how many hours you work in your home-based business; it's what you do with those hours, how you record your time, track your activities, and categorize your expenses. These are generally the same key factors that directly relate to success and profitability in the first place. You can work one hour per week or sixty hours per week in your home-based business and still achieve great success.

It's because I see this bad advice from tax preparers is one of the reasons I decided it was time to publish this book. I want to help others navigate through this and be empowered.

At the time of writing this book, I was speaking with someone who has a home-based business. This person submitted all their expenses and receipts to their tax preparer. There were tax advantages for this individual as a full-time employee and having a part-time home-based business. Unfortunately, their tax person said these home-based business write-offs are reducing their tax on their employment income too much. The tax preparer advised this person to not claim the home-based business on their taxes. This advice likely cost this individual, perhaps thousands of tax dollars that could have been a legitimate tax refund.

My goal with this book is to empower the home-based business owner to be confident in diverting these everyday expenses into a legitimate business expense, that they are recording their receipts, and allocating and tracking their time efficiently for tax purposes. But this all first starts by increasing your knowledge, getting confidence, and becoming proactive with your taxes.

There are many tax preparers who recommend that we should not do our own tax returns. While this book is not designed as a "how to" file income tax returns, its purpose is to empower you to be proactive and fully prepared for tax season. Using the services of a tax preparer may not always be in your best interest, especially if you are getting bad advice. This is why I want you to have the knowledge to empower yourself, and to take ownership of your tax write-offs. It's actually easier than you might think.

When it comes time to filing your income taxes, things are different today than they were years ago when it was all paper returns. With todays online tax websites and software, it is a fairly simple process if you have your record keeping in order knowing your annual totals with exactly what you can write-off by expense category.

But for some, they may still want the security of a tax preparer to actually file their taxes. If that's you, then you will need to know a few things about how to find the right tax person.

In finding a tax preparer it's important that they are passionate about reducing your taxes, and that they are familiar with home-based business. Are they working with any other clients in your industry? Is the tax preparer conservative and afraid of claiming write-offs to reduce your taxable income, or do they look at it as an opportunity? Many tax preparers shy away from anything they don't understand, and many unfortunately don't understand home-based business write-offs.

Other things to look for in a good tax preparer is if they are asking you questions about your home-based business situation. If they are, you can be pretty sure they are looking out for you. If your tax preparer is not asking you questions, how can they know and understand your tax situation? Your tax preparer should always be working to reduce your taxes throughout the year and as they prepare your tax return, and they should be looking to ensure you are reducing your chances of being audited.

At the end of the day you are ultimately responsible for reducing your taxes. You still have to learn enough about home-based tax write-offs and how the tax law applies to your business, so that you can use it to your benefit every minute of every day throughout the year.

If after reading this book, you find yourself thinking you or your tax preparer missed claiming some of your home-based business tax write-offs in previous years, it's still not too late. You can still file an amendment and have your past taxes adjusted. This might just be a nice financial windfall as a result of your newfound knowledge with this book, perhaps it might be worth thousands of dollars of income taxes being paid back.

Take Pam Keefe for example, she filed amendments for previous years to claim more home-based expenses that she missed. Here is what she had to say:

"...we filed 2018 taxes including home-based expenses and got a $2,000 refund. We refiled an adjustment for 2017 income tax and got $2,000 back. Refiled 2016 and got $1,800. Thanks for all the great advice!"

CHAPTER 5

Take Responsibility for Your Tax Write-Offs

There are four key concepts we need to understand in order to take responsibility for our home-based business tax write-offs. These include:

1. The history of taxation,
2. The two types of tax systems,
3. What a tax write-off really is,
4. If you don't claim it, you don't get it!

Taxes, as we know it today, existed in various forms throughout civilization. Kings, queens, chiefs, rulers, and people in authority collected taxes from the people they ruled. What was taxed, when it was taxed, and how much tax was imposed varied from society to society. Often people paid their tax bill with something they produced or gathered, such as grain, fish, minerals, or animals.

Here in North America, if we look back into history, we can see that taxation came into effect in the late 1880's, but it was not until the early 1900's when personal and corporate income taxes became legalized. This all followed the rise of Industrial America (1876-1900) that produced a new class of wealthy industrialists and a prosperous middle class.

In the United States, in 1913, the 16th Amendment was ratified, permanently legalizing income tax, called the Revenue Act of 1913. In 1917, the Canadian Parliament introduced personal income tax and corporate taxes, and in 1920, a manufacturers sales tax and other sales taxes were also introduced. This was all to help finance the First World War. During World War II, the governments introduced payroll withholding and quarterly tax payments. Since 1913, hundreds of amendments and codifications have been introduced to the taxation laws.

As time evolved the taxation system became more complicated and separation was created. This separation moved to an employee tax system which is designed to take a percentage of your income right off the top of your pay, and then a tax system for those who generate self-employed or business income. The self-employed income tax is designed as an incentive system whereby tax write-offs offer the ability to reduce taxable income through claiming expenses in the effort of earning an income.

Today, the employee tax system is what the majority of people understand. We are also now experiencing in the post COVID-19 era a "work from home" movement. Unfortunately, as the taxation system exists today, it does not offer the employee who works from home the same taxation advantages as the self-employed who works from home.

As an example, let's say you earn $2,000 and the government says that $440 must be taken off for taxes (based on a 22% tax bracket). You receive $1,560 net pay and your employer sends the $440 of income taxes directly to the government. This is what is called payroll withholding or source deductions, which became a taxation law during World War II. The government did not trust that citizens would pay the taxes themselves. The system has always been designed in such a way that the more income you earn, the higher the percentage that is taken for taxes.

The other tax system is for the self-employed or business income. It is designed in such a way that the government allows you to claim expenses (or tax write-offs) that are incurred in the effort of earning that income. When expenses are taken into account, the taxable income is reduced. So, for example, if a self-employed person earns $2,000 and has $800 in expenses, they are taxed on just $1200 in net taxable income. For those with knowledge of this system, it is an incentive system as the government wants people to start businesses and create self-employed income. As expenses increase, taxable income decreases. This system is designed to create wealth and economic growth through tax write-offs and other benefits, such as tax credits.

When it comes to those with a sole proprietorship home-based business, either part-time or full-time, it falls into the self-employed tax system. When we combine employment income and self-employed incomes together, through a home-based business, we have the opportunity to divert a percentage of personal expenses into business tax write-offs. These are the same expenses that the employee has, but as an employee you are unable to use it to bring down your taxable income.

So, if we take the above employee example where the employee earned $2,000 and paid $440 in taxes, and let's say they made no income in their part-time home-based business, but added up a portion of their everyday life expenses as tax write-offs, they can still use that amount to bring down their taxable income on their employment income. Leveraging their home-based business expenses using this method could put them in a position to get some or all of that $440 tax back from the government, by way of a tax refund.

For years I have been helping people understand this method, and it has been effective at receiving $2,000 to $10,000 in annual tax refunds from the government. Unfortunately, most people do not understand this simple tax strategy, and many who have a home-based business do not take full advantage of this. Understanding this could be one of your greatest financial breakthroughs. This is why I call it the best-kept tax secret!

Yes, I know what you are probably thinking. That your tax person will say, 'no, you can't do that!'. As the former IRS Commissioner Mark Everson once stated, "*If you don't claim it you don't get it. That's money down the drain for millions of Americans*". Perhaps you should gift this book to your tax preparer, and then claim it as a tax write-off. But remember, as I said before and will repeat again, this is not a lottery ticket. You have to take your business seriously, claim legitimate expenses, and keep accurate records.

The best part of having a home-based business is that we do get to claim all these tax write-offs against our income taxes that we cannot claim if we are just employees. Many of these are recurring expenses that we pay anyway like our home internet, cell phone, and utility bills. This is perfectly legitimate and legal; despite any bad advice you might receive from a tax preparer.

My goal in writing this book is to help you understand these tax write-offs and to ensure you are bullet-proof in your record keeping. In addition to this book, I created an online course as a deeper dive where I take you through everything in more detail and assist you in taking action with individualized one-on-one coaching. The course also includes a downloadable copy of the productivity bookkeeping system I created and have been using for the last decade that simplifies the record keeping requirements while staying compliant for tax purposes. Learn more about this course and enroll at HomeBusinessTaxSecerets.com.

As a home-based business, it's just as important to handle your personal money responsibly by knowing what income is coming in and the monthly bills going out, and then make smart decisions on spending and saving accordingly. To help with this, I have made available a template Excel spreadsheet I have been using since 2006 to manage my personal finances. Go to DougCollinsOnline.com/budget and download it for free. You will also receive a short tutorial video on how I have been using it.

When you have your finger on the financial pulse of your personal life and your home-based business, you start to look at your expenses and tax strategies a little differently. This is exactly what the big corporations do, as they make strategic investments based on their financial health and use them as tax write-off strategies.

For example, in past years I have made financial decisions during the month of December to invest in my home-based business allowing me more tax write-offs during that taxation year. I would often purchase additional office supplies (pens, paper, toner cartridges, etc.) that I know I will be needing in the months ahead. One year I made a significant investment in a training course to become certified practitioner in a complimentary field to my home-based business. I was able to claim it as a 100% tax write-off.

As I write this book, I just enrolled in a 90-day health transformation coaching system with the company I am associated with. This was an easy financial decision as it is an investment in my personal health and my ongoing home-based business success, and it's all a 100% tax write-off. These tax planning principles are what I want to help you understand and apply in your home-based business. As I said before, taxes are based on an incentive program. The government wants us to invest and in return we have the privilege of claiming it as a tax write-off expense.

To help you make great financial decisions go download the personal finances budget spreadsheet for free, you can get it at DougCollinsOnline.com/budget and be sure to watch the instructional video.

As another bonus for you, I have created a Tax Savings Estimator mobile app calculator that you can download for free at DougCollinsOnline.com/freeapp. This is a simple intuitive calculator that will instantly calculate your tax savings potential. Go download it right now and give it a try!

CHAPTER 6

Tax Write-Offs with No Business Income

There is a common misconception out there that if you never made money in your home-based business, you cannot claim it on your taxes. No income does not always mean 'no business'. Every business has to start somewhere. This is why I felt this chapter might be important to include in this book.

While it's hard to determine the average income for those with a home-based business, my research indicated that roughly 70% earn under $100,000 per year and for those who work their business on a part-time basis, that number climbs to well over 80%. In Fast Company, on July 29, 2014, an article written by Pratik Dholakiya went on to say, *"Most businesses don't make a profit until their third year and definitely not the first year"*. Mike Kappel reported in a Forbes article on March 3, 2017, that *"Many new small businesses have trouble keeping a positive net profit and few make a profit in their first year. This issue can be due to poor accounting, incorrect pricing, or lack of online marketing"*.

One of the benefits which is not focused on enough, is the potential tax write-offs that come with having a business based from home. Personally, the first two years in my current business, I received more than a $6,000 tax refund each year because of the tax write-offs I was allowed. I was still working full-time in a corporate job and was receiving employment income, in addition to claiming the tax write-offs from my part-time, home-based business.

Having a home-based business allows you to claim expenses against your employment income. The net result, when you have little or no business income in the start-up years, is that it reduces your total taxable income. This is actually a tax strategy in itself, and is one of the many reasons why I believe everyone should have a home-based business.

The difference between a bricks and mortar business and home-based businesses is that in a bricks and mortar business there is overhead expenses such rent, heat, maintenance and repairs, inventory, staff, etc. These are all direct costs to the business. When we look at a home-based business, depending on the type of business you have, there are no direct overhead costs other than some operating expenses, such as your marketing, office and education. The difference with a home-based business is that we are able to divert a percentage of our monthly living expenses into business expenses. This includes mortgage interest (or rent), utilities, internet, cell phone, home maintenance and repairs, and more.

When it comes to claiming tax write-offs with no business income, it will always come down to the ability to show an intent to make a profit, and that the business has the opportunity to earn a profit. This can be done through examples of others who have made money, showing that there is an equal opportunity for you to make money, and you need to show that it's more than just a hobby, as we covered earlier in the book. Regardless of whether or not you are earning an income in your home-based business, it's important to be tracking your business activity including your time, in order to show your intent to make a profit. If you are not keeping bullet-proof records you are leaving yourself vulnerable.

As a home-based business, we are often faced with a number of start-up expenses in the beginning. For example, in my home business for a small investment we offer a comprehensive transformational coaching system. This makes for the perfect start-up business investment, as it includes everything needed to get a business started on the track to success. Best of all, it's a 100% tax write-off as a start-up expense. These write-offs can make a significant impact on your income taxes, especially those making a part-time commitment in their home-based business while working full-time.

In the next chapter, we will go into more detail on how (why) we need to show an intent to make a profit should the home-based business not be generating a profit after expenses. But before we finish here, I wanted to expand a little more on the benefits and value of coaching since it has made such a profound impact on my business and personal development, and it does support the "intention to make a profit" we will discuss in the next chapter.

Success begins with your mind and belief system. We can learn all the different techniques, tools and sales tactics for business success, but unless we have the belief system and our self worth all in alignment, we may never actually achieve success. Or if we do reach success, it may not be lasting.

Everything began to change for me when I embraced having a coach. Having a coach helped me be accountable. A coach helped me see what my belief system was. A coach helped me reflect on what I was doing, what I was thinking, and how I was behaving. This allowed me to change that over time. I still use coaches today as I'm still going for big things. I'm transforming my life in all kinds of ways, whether it's in my home-based business, financial, my physical health, and more recently in becoming a self-published author with this book.

Until you actually get somebody to help you like this, you may continue to struggle on your own. I can tell you that you'll have more rapid success with a coach. You can get double or triple the results in less time when you have somebody supporting you and encouraging you along your path. This is why I want you to be open to, and consider, the value of a coach.

Having a coach can help you find your true passion by asking questions you may not ask yourself. A coach will guide you to the answers you know, that exist inside your heart. A coach can help you define what your goals are, develop the roadmap to create the results to get to those goals, and a coach can help you be accountable to make sure that you're taking the actions you need to take. A coach can be there for you and help you with your skills and knowledge. There's nothing like having a champion in your corner saying you can do it and believing more in you, than you might believe in yourself. A coach is somebody to make sure that you are on track, that your beliefs are all lined up so you can have, do, or be, whatever you want. This is the single most powerful thing you can do to transform your business towards financial success. I'm encouraging you to go for it.

CHAPTER 7

How (Why) to Show Intent to Make a Profit

Since you are reading this book, you are most likely taking your home-based business seriously, or at least you are open to seeing what else you are missing for tax write-offs. To answer the 'intent to make a profit' question, we typically want to differentiate between operating a hobby, or a business, something we have touched on already in this book but will go deeper into it now.

There are no concrete rules for determining if you operate a hobby or a business. But the government does say that a business must actively be trying to make a profit. So, what does all that mean? It first starts with proving your intention of operating a business with the intention to earn an income, despite a lack of income. Are you really in business or do you just treat it like a hobby, working it whenever you 'feel like it' or when it is convenient in your life? If you were the owner of a traditional bricks and mortar business and opened it when you felt like it or only when it was convenient in your life, how long would the business last? Without revenue, the overhead expenses do not get paid. This is the difference in a home-based business, as there's little to no overhead expenses.

One of the most important steps you can take to differentiate your business from a hobby is to record accurate business activities. The more records you keep, the better. You need to be able to prove that in your business you are focused on income generating activities and expenses that are in support of these activities, even if you work only a few hours per week in your business. Here are a few examples of income generating activities:

- ❏ your calendar of activities
- ❏ mileage logs
- ❏ customer lists
- ❏ prospect lists
- ❏ meeting logs and details of conversations
- ❏ records that show the amount of time (and frequency) you spent on business activities
- ❏ the kinds of tasks you did in an attempt to make your business profitable.

If you look back over the last year, what record keeping do you have to show related to your revenue-generating activities? Are you able to show marketing efforts, lead generation activities, meetings and presentation and follow-up (with whom, date and time)? All of these things are what is necessary to show an intent to make a profit from the business. If you are in a hobby, you are definitely not keeping track of all this information.

Just like it's your responsibility to know what you can and cannot write-off in your business, it's also your responsibility to proactively demonstrate that your business is valid and not a hobby.

What other business activities are you engaged in throughout the year to improve yourself? Are you taking any courses or training that can increase your knowledge, skills, and enhance your market position? Are you working with a coach or mentor? Are you participating in any marketing training, leadership events, or industry conventions? All these expenses are a 100% tax write-off.

For example, as mentioned before, in my home-based business we have business training workshops and weekly executive success coaching, as well as a mobile app to track key business and growth activities. At the end of the day, if you are going to show the government you are a legitimate business and not a hobby, you have to act like one. Actively participating in coaching and using business tools are not just an effective tax write-off strategy, they are the building blocks for long term business success and profitability.

Simply ordering this book and reading it is another activity that shows you are taking your business seriously. Any time you attend an industry-related or company training you are improving your knowledge and skills for your home-based business success. Be sure to keep a notebook or journal to record what you are learning including the date. This also becomes part of your record keeping for tax purposes.

If you have ever had a meeting with me, I have a page(s) in my notebook that records our conversation. In my business, I go through a notebook about every couple of weeks. I have storage boxes of them going back years. This also works as a great productivity tool.

I could walk anyone through a January to December daily schedule, outlining exactly what I did on any given day in my business. The notebooks show who I talked to, what we talked about, and our next steps.

The value to me is that I am able to track my business activities and I also have a detailed record going back years. This has helped me be successful in past audits and would certainly help you for tax purposes.

Here is a simple hack I have used for the last decade that can be used as a tool for your home-based business record keeping. This is not just to satisfy the government for tax purposes, it's also a great productivity tool for your business. I use a coil bound notebook from the Dollar Store. I have been using these notebooks for the last decade. I record everything in them including meetings notes, conference calls, to-do lists for the day, and any training. It acts as my complete diary. I even write my vision and monthly goals in it daily. It also makes a great productivity tool.

When I get to the end of a notebook, I'll go back to the beginning and start flipping through the pages to the end. I will see conversations I had that I forgotten about. In my new notebook I will make a list of follow-ups and start an entire new Action List. It makes an amazing follow-up tool! As Jim Rohn was known for saying, *"the fortune is in the follow-up"*.

CHAPTER 8

Tax Write-Offs as a Part-Time Business

Having a full-time employment income and a part-time home-based business can be your best scenario from a tax benefit standpoint. While your employer is withholding taxes from your pay, you can leverage your home-based business as a tax write-off, allowing you to get some (or potentially all) of your income tax money back by way of a tax refund. This tax strategy can be worth thousands and thousands of dollars! This is why I get excited to share the benefits of starting a home-based business, even from just a tax write-off perspective.

As we discussed in previous chapters, there is no defined rule from the government on the number of hours you must invest in your home-based business to actually justify it as a business. You treat it like a business, record your business activities correctly and keep simple bullet-proof records; then the government will accept any number of hours you invest in your home-based business.

When we really grasp the power of a home-based business from a tax strategy standpoint, it becomes obvious that everyone should consider this, even a part-time home-based business initially as an income tax-reduction strategy.

Just take a look at your last pay stub to see the amount of income tax that was withdrawn by your employer. Would you like to get some of that money back?

If you are working full time, you're paying taxes on that employment income. Just take a look at your last pay stub to see the amount of income tax that was withdrawn by your employer. Would you like to get some of that money back? If you answer "yes," then you'd be crazy not to have a home-based business. The simplest and most affordable, and my favorite kind of home-based businesses, is direct sales or network marketing. Once you find the right company to partner with, that offers a product or service that aligns with your values, that offers coaching, support and mentorship training, and that you can get started for a very small investment, then set-up your home office and start capturing your tax write-offs immediately. You're in business working towards your success.

These additional tax savings can help you pay off debt, invest for the future, or use it to travel. All these strategies will be covering in the next few chapters.

CHAPTER 9

Tax Deferral Investments vs Tax Write-Offs

Financial Planners and banking institutions love tax season as it's the height of their busy season for selling tax deferral investment products like RRSP's. We've often heard the financial experts say: "the ability to deduct your RRSP contribution from taxable income is a significant advantage."

In this chapter we will take a closer look at the tax benefits of these investment products as it compares to starting a home-based business, and how we can use both together for an even greater financial advantage. I am all for investment products myself. I included this in the book because I want to highlight that a home-based business is often overlooked and very few truly understand that this is also an effective tax strategy.

While I totally believe tax deferral investments do make financial sense, you need to have the cash up front to invest.

For some, this might be a challenge. Since it is a tax deferral investment you will receive an immediate tax benefit, but at some point, in the future you will pay tax when the money is withdrawn. In my experience, as we discussed earlier, a home-based business can create immediate tax refunds against employment income, then that money can be used to invest in tax deferral investment. This is where the two strategies can be used for the best of both worlds. We will get into more detail on that in the next chapter. This is an important tax strategy, so I decided to cover it with its own chapter.

When we invest in tax deferral investments, it will provide an immediate tax benefit; but we have to be prepared to invest for the long term. This can be the downside as your money becomes volatile to the market. When the market crashes, your investment value goes down with it. The plan is to ride it out.

Over the last decade I have used these tax deferral investment products in combination with my home-based business tax write-offs with great success. I have been fortunate to have a great financial planner to learn from who understands home-based business, as he also works from home. This strategy has saved me hundreds of thousands in tax dollars. Throughout this time period, I have watched my investment dollars fluctuate with the market, but I have continued to focus on the long-term growth.

If you are considering putting money in a tax deferral investment product, it is important to consider your-long term goals and financial ability to invest long-term, weathering any market fluctuations.

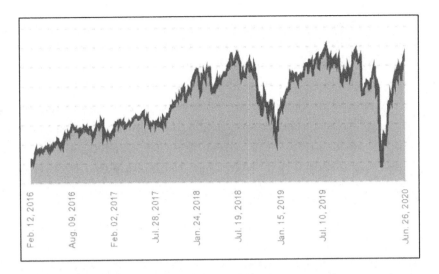

This graph is an actual trend showing one of my investment products over the last four years. Here's a recent example of market fluctuations, as a result of the COVID pandemic in early 2020, where the market literally crashed overnight. You can see the big drop in value near the end of the graph and then a few months later it came back up in value more than it was at any point in the last four years. It will be interesting to watch it going forward.

Most financial advisors, bankers, and tax preparers are familiar with the tax deferral investment products as a tax strategy, but they know very little (or nothing) about home business write-offs. I believe using them both has been one of my greatest financial advantages. This can also be yours, especially if you work full-time and have a part-time home-based business. This is why I am so passionate about educating and training those who are open to learning about the tax savings power of a home-based business.

The biggest challenge with investment products is that you need the cash to invest in the first place. When we operate a business from home, there are so many monthly expenses we can legitimately divert from a personal expense to a business tax write-off. In Section Two of this book we will go into more detail on these expenses specifically, but they do add up quickly and create a significant tax advantage without needing to come up with additional cash investment to generate that tax write-off.

After earning an income, paying incomes taxes and all the monthly bills, it's suggested that ten percent be left to invest each month. But for many it's just the opposite. So many are going into debt each month hoping something will change. Which group are you? Who do you know in this latter group? And what are their options for any change?

For most people saving and investing does not really start to happen until their kids are out of college when most adults are well into their 50s. Starting to invest at age 50 only leaves about 20 years for wealth accumulation. In the next chapter I will take you through a proven and effective 3 to 5-year financial plan leveraging home-based tax write-offs and tax deferral investment products that could significantly impact your financial situation.

CHAPTER 10

What You Should Do with Your Tax Refund

In the last chapter we covered the benefits of leveraging tax deferral investment strategies and home-based tax write-offs. Now that we understand this, it's time to begin building our plan to create financial security leveraging these two tax strategies.

Over the last decade I have coached many home-based business owners to find, and claim, their tax write-offs. I watched them save on average from $2,000 to $10,000 in taxes, often receiving it as a tax refund. I then watched them spend that money on things that offered no additional financial or tax benefit. This is why I decided to include this chapter, because it is important and deserves your consideration. I also want to show you a simple wealth-building formula using your tax refund as part of the strategy.

When it comes to receiving a tax refund as a result of claiming these home-based write-offs, I recommend reviewing your financial priorities before spending it on "desires and wants." If the money can be used to pay down high-interest debt like credit cards, that might be a great option, as long as this does not free up that credit so that you can spend again.

More importantly, consider how this tax refund can be utilized to create new tax refunds the following the year. I like to recommend you look at investing that money into a tax deferral investment product that creates compound interest on your money, and offers a tax receipt for that taxation year, further increasing your tax benefits, and continuing to maximize your home-based tax write-offs – a double benefit.

In all of these situations you are using your tax refund to create new legitimate tax write-offs and compounding your tax benefits year-to-year. When this strategy is used effectively over a 3 to 5-year period this could be your ticket to reducing or paying off debts, and significantly increasing your financial nest egg. I have used this strategy over the last decade saving six figures in income tax and leveraging it to create even more tax savings.

The other strategy is to consider investing some of your tax refund into your home-based business, allowing you to claim that as a tax write-off. Examples of this might be a business trip or training related to your business (refer to Chapter 15). You might want to invest in a new laptop and use that as a tax write-off as a home office expense (refer to Chapter 12). Or perhaps you can do some upgrades, maintenance and repairs to your home, allowing you to claim a percentage of the expense as a tax write-off (refer to Chapter 11).

Knowledge In Action

Business Use of Home Expenses

In my experience the business use of home is one area that most business owners are either not set up correctly to maximize their tax write-offs or they are just not fully taking advantage of it.

Home-based business owners are eligible to claim "operating expenses" just like any other business. Earlier in the book I shared my experience operating a bricks & mortar business. The difference between that kind of business and a home-based business is that the expenses we claim are what we are spending to operate our place of residence, such as:

- mortgage interest (or rent if you lease)
- heat and electricity.
- home insurance
- lawn care
- snow removal
- property taxes
- maintenance and repairs.

We can claim these home-based business expenses as long as our home office (and storage area) space meets three requirements:

1. It is used as your primary place of business,
2. It is used exclusively for your business,
3. You regularly work there.

When you meet these three requirements, you can begin claiming your home expenses. Once you have established your home office inside your home, you will want to calculate the square footage measurements of that dedicated office space as a percentage of your total house square footage.

The way the calculation works is to first calculate the total amount of living space in your home. It is important to note that living space does not have to include hallways, bathrooms, closest, and stairways. These are not "living spaces" in your home but are considered travel and storage areas. By using this adjusted living space calculation, you are decreasing the

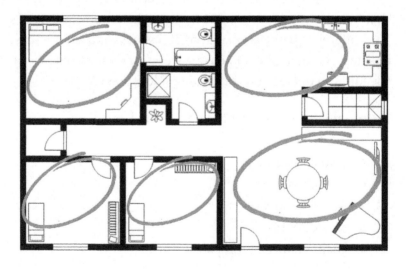

overall square footage of your home, therefore, increasing the percentage of your home office.

This is perfectly within the government tax guidelines for home office. In Canada, the CRA states "*use a reasonable basis*" and in the US the IRS states *"to the percentage of the home floor space used for business"* for calculating business use of home amount. What might be a red flag for an audit would be claiming a very high percentage of your home-based office as a total square footage of your home.

For example, let's say your setting up a desk in your living room and plan to claim that entire room as your home office, thinking that would be the largest percentage of square footage since that is the largest room in your home. If you were ever audited, this might become a red flag as the government would suspect this room is not exclusive for business. They know you have to live there also, that's why it's called a living room.

But even if it is exclusive and your primary location for doing business you would have to have it well documented through your record keeping. This would include activities in the office such as a history of business-related appointments, sales calls and personal development such as training. Without record keeping on these activities there's a possibly the business will appear to be a hobby and wasn't really taken all that seriously throughout the year, the claim may be denied. As we covered so far in this book, there are lots of tell-tale signs on a tax return that a home business might be a hobby.

Mortgage vs Lease

While most people believe owning the home where they live is better, when you operate a home-based business there are tax considerations. When you own your home with a mortgage, you can only claim a portion of the mortgage interest not the mortgage payment. This is more valuable in the early years of a mortgage, since most of your payments go towards interest. When comparing that to a lease, you can claim a percentage of the lease payment.

For some, a lease can provide other benefits, such as flexibility related to where you live and how long. You can also invest the money you would use for a down payment into something like an RRSP - that will provide a tax relief. I went through this calculation myself in late 2019 when selling our home after 13 years and relocating to another province. For us, considering where we are in life, that I work from home full-time and we are relocating to another province, it made sense from a financial and taxation standpoint to rent where we live for now.

Maintenance and Repairs

Another area that can offer tax savings is the ability to claim a percentage of maintenance and repairs on your home. For example, if I painted my office, that is a 100% tax deduction. It is not prorated over the full house. But anything else inside or outside of the home is prorated based on the square footage. As we discussed earlier, often when we lease, these expenses are very minimal as maintenance and repairs become the landlord's responsibility.

From a home owner's perspective, we often do spring cleaning and planting in our yards, including topsoil and seed for our grass. As a home-based business, we can include that as a home maintenance expense. One time the motor stopped working in my home air exchanger, which cost $500 for the replacement including servicing. I included a prorated amount of that expense to my home-based business as a tax write-off. If I did not have a home-based business, that expense would not be a tax write-off at all, and it would be paid for with after-tax income.

By having a home-based business, there are just so many opportunities to claim expenses around your home as a legitimate tax write-off.

CHAPTER 12

Home Office Supplies

Office supplies are the tangible, traditional office items used up by the business. The government allows home-business owners to deduct 100 percent of these items as a tax write-off. Office operating expenses can include:

- Web site services, cloud services
- Monthly costs services internet hosting fees
- Software, including web-based software
- Merchant account service fees
- Desktop computers, laptops, iPads, and tablets
- Consumable items (see list on next page)

There are so many different items within your household that, if you're operating a business from home, you can claim but could not without a home-based business. Things like that new coffee maker you purchased to drink coffee in your office. Yes, you can actually claim that coffee maker, the coffee you drink in your office and your coffee filters. Everything has to be directly related to your home-based business.

For larger value purchases, like business equipment, computers, and office furniture your local taxation laws have guidelines on how this is depreciated as a "business asset", as you may not be able to write it off all in the year it is purchased. This amount usually runs around $500 or more per one item, such as a laptop. The reason for this is that the government knows you will be using these larger items over a few years.

Office supplies is a catch-all term of expenses that fall into low-cost, often consumable business purchases. The list is quite long and very extensive. Here's a list of a few items that are a 100 percent tax write-off to your business:

Bathroom Tissue	Invoices
Batteries	Kleenex
Beverages	Knives
Blades	Light Bulbs
Books	Magazines
Boxes	Mops
Brooms	Organizers
Business Cards	Paper Clips
Business Equipment	Paper Towel
Calendars	Pens & Pencils
Cards	Plants
Cleaning Supplies	Postage
Clip Boards	Postage Stamps
Coffee & Filters	Post-It Notes
Computer Accessories	Printer Cartridges
Curtains	Printer Paper
Directories	Rubber Bands
Dust Covers	Rulers
Envelopes	Signage
Erasers	Snacks & Drinks

Fasteners   Soap
File Folders   Software
Fire Extinguisher Stapler
First Aid Kid   Stationary
Flashlight   Storage Shelving
Forms & Labels   Tape & Dispenser
Garbage Bags   Wall Decorations
Greeting Cards   Water
Hole Puncher   Wrist Supports

CHAPTER 13

Your Personal Vehicle is a Business Expense

Vehicle mileage is another one of those under claimed of all home-based tax write-offs. It can also be the number one red flag for an audit. Perhaps that's why so many shy away from it.

According to US News article by Maryalene LaPonsie, dated March 16, 2020, "*You need to know the rules for claiming mileage on your taxes and, more importantly, you need to keep careful records*". It was also stated in The Globe & Mail, in an article by Augusta Dwyer on July 23, 2017, that *"tracking business mileage is important, yet few keep a mileage log"*. The Financial Post article by Jamie Golombek dated September 14, 2018 reported that, *"automobile expenses continue to be an area of scrutiny for the taxman, so you shouldn't be surprised if the government starts asking you questions about how you may have claimed any vehicle expenses"*.

It took me years to finally get some discipline in tracking my personal vehicle expenses and claiming business mileage. I always kept copies of my expense receipts for gas, vehicle registration and repairs. But when it came time to knowing what exactly was my business vs personal mileage, I had no accurate mileage records.

This is most often one of the areas that home-based entrepreneurs fail to report completely and accurately. I have seen many leave this out of claiming on their taxes altogether and others put in their best guess. In this chapter, we will go through the most common and simplified method for tracking and claiming your business mileage for tax purposes. We will also do a comparison on the difference of purchasing or leasing a personal vehicle, from a home-based business tax perspective.

When it comes to business mileage record keeping, the government expects you to keep detailed records including:

- ❏ The date of the business trip
- ❏ The purpose of the business trip and destination
- ❏ The distance travelled to/from home

You will need to have the total mileage driven for the year, so make sure you have written down your starting mileage at the beginning of the year and the mileage at the end of the year.

The total miles driven for business purposes will be a percentage of the total mileage for the year. This is the percentage calculation you will use for all your vehicle expenses throughout the year.

What most tax preparers recommend is to get yourself one of those little mileage books at the office supply store and keep it in your car. Although the intention of using it is there, I've not met many people who have consistently used it over an extended period of time. There are also mileage tracker apps that are available for those who are a little more "techie". Whatever you decide to use, it's important to be consistent and keep accurate records.

Here is what I have been doing for years, and it has worked very well for me. I record all my business activity in my calendar on my laptop, and that syncs to my cell phone calendar. So, for example, if I have a meeting or do an errand that is business related, it is recorded in my calendar with specifics including date, time, and location. I have learned to manage my life around my calendar. I am in the habit of scheduling everything, whether it's personal or business. This allows me to plan my weeks and be productive and efficient in my life and business on a daily basis.

Then at the end of the year, I export my entire calendar for the previous year into an Excel file. Once I have everything in an Excel file, I sort through all my calendar activities and identify what was business related. I then have a list of all business-related activities with details that meet the tax requirements.

Once I have this list, I add the mileage for each. This can be easily done through an online driving distance website online. I just add the mileage up, and it gives me the total for the year that is business. Since I know my total mileage driven for the year, I can easily calculate the percentage of it as business from the total. This is the exact method I teach inside the HomeBusinessTaxSecrets.com course. I actually take you through one of my vehicle mileage reports, and show you how

I used it to calculate my business mileage and record my expenses. I have been doing this for years and it's very simple and effective, and audit proof.

You are eligible to deduct a percentage of your car expenses from your business. These expenses are the same whether you lease or buy your car. These expenses include the following:

1. Loan Interest (or lease payment)
2. Fuel
3. Maintenance and repairs
4. Insurance
5. License and registration
6. Parking and tolls

When it comes to your ability to calculate a write-off amount on your vehicle there are two methods - purchase or lease.

Let's say that 50% of the mileage driven for the year was business related. Here is how it looks before we factor in the vehicle payment.

Expense Item	Yearly Total	50% Business
Fuel	$2,500	$1,250
Maint. & Repairs	$1,200	$600
Insurance	$1,500	$750
Licence & Reg.	$250	$125
Parking & Tolls	$100	$50
Tax Write-Off	$5,550	**$2,775**

Lease or Finance Your Vehicle

For comparison purposes, let's take a look at the lease vs. finance payments to provide some clarity either way. I will use a fictitious list of vehicle expenses for our comparison purposes. When leasing your vehicle, you can claim the business percentage of your lease payments. For example, using 50% business mileage, if your lease payment is $400 per month, then you can claim $200 per month for a total for $2,400 per year.

When you purchase your vehicle or take out a loan, you can claim the percentage (using this sample example of 50% business mileage) of the interest portion, and the government provides the tax rules on how you can claim depreciation as a percentage of the vehicle value each year, as a tax write-off against your home-based business. Keep in mind this amount continues to decline as the vehicle gets older.

Most online tax software can help you easily calculate this amount, or your tax preparer will know how to take care of this. But for illustration purposes, let's say it is 30% of the value.

For example, let's say you just purchased a vehicle valued at $30,000 over a 48-month term at 4% interest. You would be paying approximately $625 interest per year. You can claim 50% of that $625 interest (using the 50% business mileage as our example). To then calculate the business write-off for the value of the vehicle, let's say it is 30%. $30,000 x 30% is $9,000.

The following chart shows how the comparison of tax write-off from a lease to purchase.

Expense Item	Lease (at 50%)	Purchase (at 50%)
Fuel	$1,250	$1,250
Maint. & Repairs	$600	$600
Insurance	$750	$750
Licence & Reg.	$125	$125
Parking & Tolls	$50	$50
Vehicle Payments	$2,400	see below
Interest (loan)	---	$312.50
Tax Write-Off	**$5,175**	**$3,087.50**

The Vehicle Payments amount for Purchase would include a vehicle depreciation amount for this comparison purposes. If you were doing this for the purchase of a new vehicle the total write-off would be comparable, however as the vehicle ages the depreciation amount continues to decline, whereas with a lease it is based on a percentage of the ongoing payment.

Leasing is often suggested for business use, but for those of us in a home-based business, it depends on the percentage of personal versus business mileage driven. In this example we compared 50% personal vs. business mileage, but if you are part-time in your home-based business your mileage would likely be much lower, not offering as great a tax write-off amount.

CHAPTER 14

Meals & Entertainment for Business

This can be one of the most enjoyable of expense categories, but also one that can lead us into audit trouble if we are not careful. For meals and entertainment to be justified as a business expense, it must meet three criteria:

1. Have an opportunity to generate income
2. Create goodwill
3. Thank customers or associates for a job well done

When it comes to meals and entertainment as a business expense, we can always discuss business everywhere we go. Whether it's coffee, a meal, or some other entertainment situation, as long as it meets these criteria, it can be expensed. The cost cannot be "lavish or extravagant". To effectively claim it as a business expense, business must have been discussed. Always be sure to keep a record of who you were with and what was discussed. Your travel mileage is also a business expense if you use your vehicle.

When it comes to claiming entertainment expenses, the tax laws are different in Canada and the United States. As of the time of writing this book, the IRS will not allow most entertainment expenses for such activities such as golf memberships or sporting events to be used to entertain clients. My guess is that we might see a change during this post COVID-19 era, as a way to stimulate the economy and get businesses spending money again.

But generally speaking, as a home-based business, we can claim meals as long as we are keeping track of them, including who we met with and what was discussed. This can include any current client or potential client, including family members or friends. The important thing to remember is accurate record keeping.

We can claim 50% of our meals and entertainment as a business expense. The important thing to remember is that this expense has to be business related, which can be a gray area as it doesn't take much to have a conversation with someone about your home-based business.

This is a category that is under-utilized by many who have a home-based business. It does have flexibility because if you go out and have a meal with somebody, be strategic by making sure you have a conversation about business, but do it in a professional way. In our business workshop training, we teach the skills to do this professionally with confidence without coming across like a sales person with a hidden agenda.

CHAPTER 15

Travel & Education

When it comes to business travel, it is a 100% tax write-off. As someone who enjoys travel and personal development, I get really excited about this one. This would include the cost of transportation for you and your luggage to/from your destination, lodging such as hotel, your meals and entertainment expenses, cost of transportation while away from home like a car rental and any other reasonable incidental expenses.

One of the most underutilized tax write-offs I have seen in home-based business is leveraging a business trip combined with personal time and using the entire expense as a tax write-off. I have met many who do this but fail to keep accurate records of their expenses, leaving themselves vulnerable if ever audited.

Here's a general rule to follow when combining business and vacation. If your trip is primarily for business (more than half of the days are for business) the cost of the round trip is a full tax write-off. So, when you do it right, you can take vacations around business trips and claim it all as a tax write-off. This is another reason I enjoy my home-based business as the business offers flexibility and the unlimited geography or territory to expand business relationships and that will grow your business at the same time.

Through my home-based business I have had the fortune of travelling all over North America and as far away as the Philippines claiming these trips as a tax write-off. This simple tax strategy has allowed me to tack on stays at beach resorts on the Gulf Coast, travelled to San Francisco to tour Alcatraz prison (a lifetime bucket list item now checked off), as well as staying in some of the most luxurious resorts and hotels.

Doug Collins is with Allyssa Collins and 2 others at Toronto Pearson International Airport.
June 26, 2013 · Mississauga, ON · 🌐 ▾

Here we go! On board Philippine Airlines flight 119 to Manila with arrival on Friday morning at 8am local time. Good bye for now!

While I enjoyed myself personally, I always conducted business on these trips; often they were scheduled around a company convention or a business training event.

The rule is to always make sure you put in business time while away and be intentional with your business. A business day while away does not require you to do business all day. Here are some general guidelines:

1. Any day you put in at least four hours of work is considered a business day
2. Any day your presence is required, for any amount of time, it's a business day
3. Your travel days count as business days.

When my children were young and participating in sports, we often had to go away on the weekends for competitions and tournaments. I always planned ahead, set-up a few meetings in that area and then claimed the vehicle mileage, hotel, and my personal meals as a business expense.

Keep in mind that the government always wants to be sure that your business trip is not a vacation in disguise. You want to be sure you can prove the trip wasn't just a personal vacation. So, keep detailed records of why you were there and who you met with. Keep an accurate record of all your expenses. Inside the HomeBusinessTaxSecrets.com course you will receive a travel expense summary template, to organize all these expenses in an itemized format for the entire trip and keep all the receipts together for that one trip.

I created this travel expense summary template to know what the business trip cost, the investment I made in my business, and how it financially impacted me as a tax write-off. This template helps make good financial decisions. If I travelled to attend a conference or event, I would want to know what my entire investment was including airline tickets, hotel and meals. This is just good business practice and shows the government you take your business seriously.

As a business, you should be constantly investing in sharpening your skills. If you purchase a training course, attend a conference, or even a networking event, you can add the expense as a tax write-off when you file taxes. You could deduct costs for business magazines, professional journals, and educational books like this book. Yes, the cost of this book you are reading right now is a 100% tax write-off for you.

To determine if you can deduct a training and education expense, decide if the expense is both ordinary and necessary to your home-based business. The government requires it to be ordinary if it is common and accepted in your industry and necessary if it is helpful and appropriate for your business. If they are and the expense does qualify, you can write them off from your taxes.

Having a home-based business afforded me the opportunity to attend many conferences and training course throughout North America. This has allowed me to personally connect with some of the greatest in their field from speakers, authors, and even Olympic athletes. In every instance, it has been 100% tax write-offs as travel and education expenses.

Doug Collins is at Green Valley Ranch Resort Spa & Casino.
May 19, 2012 Henderson, NV, United States

Brendon Burchard ...#1 New York Times best selling author. Check out his new book "The Charge" and his web-site High Performance Academy.

CHAPTER 16

Marketing & Advertising

Marketing and Advertising is a very broad category, so it covers many areas related to the promotion of your business. Since this is a very broad category it can be a gray area in the tax rules, but it has to be an ordinary and necessary business expense for the size and your type of home-based business.

Any expense you incur in this category has to be with the proper intent to promote your business, create brand awareness and is an opportunity to grow your revenue. Marketing is a broad term that indicates advertising, promotion, entertainment, you name it. Most marketing expenses are fully 100% deductible.

This would generally include expenses for business activities such as:

- Advertising in various media.
- Marketing activities such as direct mail.

- Promotional expenses, such as sponsorship of events and promotional items for giveaways, i.e., shirts, pens, product samples.
- Online activities such as social media advertising and SEO services.
- Costs of producing advertising materials such as business cards, brochures, and web sites.
- Costs of advertising and/or hosting special promotional events.

Always be sure to keep good records of your marketing activities and the expenses including any receipts or invoices.

If you are in a product based direct sales or network marketing business, you can claim your monthly personal usage of the product as a marketing expense. The general rule you can use is to claim 50% of your personal monthly use. To support this tax write-off, it's important to have documentation of legitimate intent to grow your sales, to create customer awareness, and to create brand awareness using your personal use purchases. This can be as simple as keeping track of who you give product samples to, your follow-up and tracking the results. From a business success standpoint, it is important to know how this is working.

Another fun tax strategy to leverage is hosting small meetings in your home or other locations. I have done this in years past where I would include some food, beverages and product samples. This entire expense falls under marketing, and not meals and entertainment. If it is directly related to an event, opportunity presentation or offer, then it falls under a promotional expense and it's 100% tax write-off. The government says your business can reasonably deduct the cost of goodwill advertising to keep your name in front of your clients.

When I work with business partners to start-up their business in my company, I show them how to take their initial investment and use it as a tax write-off. This then allows them to make the investment as a 100% tax write-off and then get their business off to a running start.

In today's rapidly changing world there are so many creative and legitimate ways to market your home-based business that offer you significant tax write-offs, without breaking the bank on expenses.

One creative way of marketing that is mostly ignored today is mailing handwritten cards. I first learned this watching my dad, Ron Collins, as a young boy. Dad used cards to touch so many lives. I remember he would always have stacks of cards on his desk every day ready to go out in the mail.

This is a picture of my Dad taken in his home office circa 1998. Sadly, he passed away in 2002 at the young age of 66. I was 33 years old at the time. I truly owe my entrepreneurial spirit and drive for success to my dad.

I recall at Dad's funeral the Pastor asking for everyone who had ever received a card from my Dad to please stand up, and in that packed church everyone stood up. My dad spent three decades of his career sending get-well cards, birthday cards, anniversary cards and thank you cards. I share this simple strategy as we could all learn and apply this in our home-based business.

There's only been one other person I have personally met who has been as consistent and dedicated to sending cards as my Dad. That is Darlene Long who wrote the foreword in this book. She has been a great coach, mentor, friend, and business partner, even a grandmother figure to my kids.

In 2017, Darlene was awarded the prestigious Mark of Distinction Award from the Direct Sellers Association of Canada (DSA). This is an annual award to recognize a home-based business leader who upholds the values of trust and integrity, and who exhibits leadership qualities that inspire others to achieve their full potential. Darlene was chosen from more than fifty DSA member companies, representing close to one million home-based distributors across Canada. This speaks volumes to her core-values and long standing three-decade uninterrupted tenure with our company.

One of the more memorable cards I ever received from Darlene was a "Happy Retirement" card when I left corporate America and started my home-based business on a full-time basis.

This card stands out for me as it was a significant turning point in my life. That was in January 2011, and since then I have received many cards from her that I have always treasured.

Sending cards can make a significant impact in the lives of others and keep you top of mind, and it's at a minimal cost. Think about it, when was the last time you received a hand written card as a follow-up from a meeting or when you purchased something. In this post COVID-19 era we are finding our mailboxes empty as the world becomes more digital. Perhaps it's time we go back to the days of the hand written card with a heartfelt note of appreciation that is received in that empty mailbox.

From a tax write-off standpoint, it impacts so many areas of your home-based business as it is a 100% tax write-off, it shows "intent to make a profit", and could be a key to growing your business.

CHAPTER 17

Manage Your Inventory

This chapter is for you if you carry inventory that is held for sales in the normal course of business. This includes raw materials purchased that will be used in finished goods. If you have a business where you do carry inventory, there's just one level of an additional calculation, which is quite easy. Here we will touch on an overview of some of the bookkeeping requirements for tracking and recording inventory, to keep your financials and for tax purposes. This is called the cost of goods sold.

It is important to note that there are situations when you can write off your inventory as a business expense. These could be situations when you use some of your inventory for things such as customer demos, samples, or a promotional giveaway. This is where your inventory then becomes an expense in the marketing and advertising category, as covered in the previous chapter.

Only the costs of goods that were actually sold can be deducted as a business expense for inventory. It is important to keep accurate records and record these numbers if you carry inventory in your home-based business because the cost of goods sold may be one of your largest assets in your home-based business, next to your computer, office equipment, and furnishings.

It is a three-step procedure to accurately calculate the Cost of Goods Sold:

1. You start with the cost of your inventory on hand at the beginning of the year or when you started your business, if this is a new venture.
2. You add all the inventory purchases during the year. Beginning inventory plus your purchases during the year, gives you a total inventory available for sale during the year.
3. At the end of the year you will need to make a list of inventory on-hand. Then you subtract the ending inventory value and the total inventory available for sale. The resulting value is your Cost of Goods Sold.

Not all home-based businesses require inventory. For example, today most companies in the network marketing profession handle all the inventory, packaging, ecommerce, logistics and tracking. For most network marketing companies there is start-up investment, but it is typically a smaller amount and is based on a personal consumption of product. This is not necessarily inventory. It is a direct business expenses and is a tax write-off that falls under marketing and advertising, (refer to Chapter 19).

CHAPTER 18

Other Expenses

Accounting & Legal Fees: You can claim any legal fees if you hired legal counsel or fees paid to have your income taxes prepared and filed.

Associations: Any memberships fees paid for trade associations or networking related organizations that are business related are a tax write-off.

Business Licences, Memberships & Subscriptions: You can deduct annual licence fees, memberships, subscriptions to trade publications and other business-related associations.

Capital Expenditures: Any large purchases you make, such as a desk, computer, or large office equipment follows the tax guidelines for depreciation.

Charitable Donation: You can write off expenses for donations. What qualifies for charitable giving is the following: cash donations, property such as inventory or equipment, and sponsorship of local charity events.

Children on Payroll: You can pay your children wages to work for you in your home-based business, and they do not have to file income or declare the wages as a taxable income. This is specific to children under the age of 18 and a certain amount of income depending on your country, which changes from year to year. The amount can be in the rage of $6,000 to $10,000 per year, or more.

Cleaning Services: Any cleaning or housekeeping services you pay for can be a tax write-off. This would be prorated to the percentage of your home office, as calculated in business use of home expenses in Chapter 11. If the cleaning was only for your home-office area then it is 100%.

Clothing: Generally clothing is not an expense write-off unless it is branded with your company logo, slogan or product advertisement.

Coaching & Consulting: Hiring a coach or consultant is a 100% tax write-off, as long as it can be directly related to your business.

Contract Labor: This includes all fees paid to independent contractors. For example, if you hired a graphic designer to design a logo or a web developer to create your website, their fees are a 100% tax write-off.

Commissions & Product Sales: You are required to report all sales, including product sales to customers and your total monthly commissions paid to others.

Freelancers: Whenever you hire a freelancer to do work for you these costs are a tax write-off expense.

Gifts & Customer Samples: You can claim any expenses related to gifts and samples to customers as a tax write-off. These can include gift cards, flowers, etc.

Insurance: Some home businesses require special insurance. If you incurred any business-related insurance such as liability or special homeowner's insurance, you can claim this. This does not include regular home, vehicle or life insurance.

Interest & Bank Fees: If you had any interest or bank fees that you paid that are specifically related to your business, you can claim it as a business expense.

Moving Expenses: Moving expenses can be claimed based on the prorated percentage of your home-based business. This is the same calculation used in Chapter 11.

Online Courses: Any courses or training you take, that advance your skills in your business is a tax write-off. For example, taking my HomeBusinessMoneySecrets.com course is a tax write-off, and it also shows your intention to take your business seriously. The students who take this course average a ten to thirty-times return on their investment.

Parties: Business parties, lunches or events that are organized to promote the business, fall under entertainment expenses. If you are in a business that requires people to gather at home or do meetings, this becomes a great area to create expenses.

Sales tax: As a small home-based sole proprietorship, sales tax paid on goods purchased for inventory and any operating expense are included. Sales taxes are collected from customers based on the government guidelines. As an example, in Canada any business with gross sales over $30,000 is required to charge tax and remit to the government on a quarterly or annual basis.

Start-up Costs: Start-up costs are those expenses incurred leading up to the launch of the business. This is often different from the operating expenses once the business has started. Most governments have a financial limit on what can be claimed as a start-up cost, to be written off in the first year of business. As mentioned previously in this book, the enrollment investment in a network marketing business, for example, can be claimed as a start-up cost and written off a 100% tax deduction. This can offer a significant tax benefit as if you had full-time employment and enrolled into a network marketing business as a part-time home-based business.

Storage Area: In addition to your home office calculation from Business Use of Home Expenses in Chapter 11, if you find that you keep extra storage of business items in your home, you can add this storage to your square footage calculation.

This Book: The money you paid for this book is a 100% tax write-off. In fact, you can create even more tax write-offs by purchasing additional copies and gift them to your business partners who also have a home-based business.

SECTION THREE

Next Steps

CHAPTER 19

Calculating Your Tax Savings Potential

This is one of the chapters in this book that I am most excited about. The topic of leveraging a home-based business to pay less income tax has been something I have talked about for the last two decades. As we discussed throughout this book, even a part-time business working only a few hours per week can have a significant benefit of lowering your taxable employment income.

It is widely known that many of those who do have a home-based business are not taking advantage of every tax strategy. In fact, in my last decade's experience, I have met very few people who are taking advantage of every home-based tax write-off, and I have also met many who are leaving themselves vulnerable to audits. I hope from reading this book, you have discovered some great tax strategies yourself that you can use and the importance of record keeping.

Whenever I spoke to someone about these tax write-off benefits, I always gave rough figures as a best guess on potential tax savings based on a particular set of questions. I then wondered if there would be a way that I could come up with a calculation that was simple and easy and could be used to take this conversation to a new level, in order to really show someone their tax savings potential.

I took on this project running some calculations starting with my own personal tax returns, and then talking to others as my test subjects. I finally figured out the calculations. After extensive research, I finally came up with a very simple mobile app that I called the Tax Savings Estimator.

This Tax Savings Estimator is a very intuitive calculator where you enter just six numbers and two percentages. It will then instantly calculate your tax savings. Inside this app we calculate the following:

1. Monthly Home Expenses
2. Monthly Vehicle Expenses
3. Annual Travel & Education Expenses
4. Monthly Meals & Entertainment Expenses
5. Monthly General Office Expenses
6. Monthly Marketing & Advertising Expenses

These are not the only tax write-offs we can claim by having a home-based business. As you have learned here in the previous chapters, there are so many more. But I wanted to focus on the main ones to give others an idea of the tax savings involved! I wanted to use it in my own business as a tool to help others understand the financial impact, based on their own circumstances.

If you are in a home-based business where you recruit and develop others to build a business themselves, such as direct sales or network marketing, this App is a great tool to use as part of your presentation showing your prospects their tax saving potential with their own home-based business.

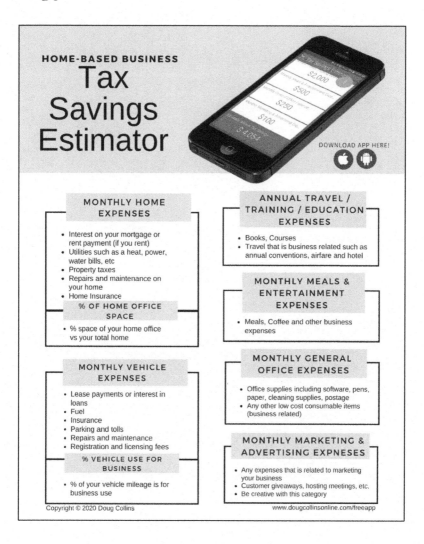

To download the Tax Savings Estimator mobile app visit DougCollinsOnline.com/freeapp and you'll also receive an instructional PDF and video tutorial.

CHAPTER 20

Pulling It All Together

We have come a long way in this book, and now you've learned many of the tax write-offs available for the home-based business. It's now time for you to apply this knowledge and these tax strategies into a simple and effective audit-proof record keeping system. Remember, the biggest reason we don't claim all these write-offs is because of the lack of accurate record keeping and the fear of losing in an audit. The truth is, your tax department likes backup and record keeping. I like to call this "being audit-proof". I can't express the importance of this often enough!

Following a simple system and maintaining accurate bullet-proof records will be the key to being audit-proof. This is where the HomeBusinessTaxSecrets.com course will show you how to simplify record keeping and improve business productivity. It's a system of paperwork that takes very little time at the end of each month. That time investment each month combined with your new found knowledge will give you returns of thousands of dollars each year on your taxes.

This online course is nine self-paced video lessons covering everything you need to know about home-based business expenses, bullet-proof record keeping, and capturing all your legitimate tax write-offs; so, you can start reducing your income tax right away.

Here's what others are saying:

Jackie Lee
June 19 at 7:08 PM

I'd like to say thank you to Doug for helping me with a year of tax report. I was feeling lost and tried to find some professionals to help me but all they did was just send me a document for me to fill in when I had no idea where even to start.

I was very lucky and happy to find Doug and taking his course to build the good starting point then Doug was always a message or an email away whenever I needed any clarifications or support. His module certainly helped me to clarify year long of back tracking. It wasn't easy but it was totally doable for me as first time tax reporter for my husband's small company.

I would like to recommend Doug to anyone who needs extra help and support with their taxes. He really walked with me through the whole process and I saved more than $2,000 at least!

Thank you again Doug. I will spread the news to more people so that they could get the right help from the start. 😊

Darlene Long
February 16

It's about time there's a course that helps people claim every write-off they are entitled to as a home-based business. These strategies are golden! This will help everyone find all their tax deductions more effectively.

Patricia Creighton Thanks Doug for all your help! Brian and I appreciate your patience and willingness to answer our MANY questions. 😊 The course is very well laid out. We like the video format and love the Excel monthly tracking sheet. So excited about our thousands of dollars in tax savings. Thanks again!!

Like · Reply · 11w   👍 1

Judy Gilman shared a link.
🔾 Admin · August 20, 2019

I purchased this online tax course from Doug Collins, who is a fellow coach and I highly recommend it. Worth the inexpensive price to enable you to do your bookkeeping correctly for a small business like ours. I encourage you to check it out and consider ordering it. Each session is short, informative and will save you money and headaches come tax season!

Elsie Roman
April 20

I just got off the phone with Doug Collins. I highly recommend you give him a call if you have any tax questions. So good or join his tax course he's offering. I appreciate all the gold nuggets I received today.
Thanks Doug.

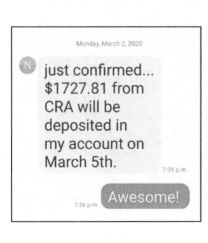

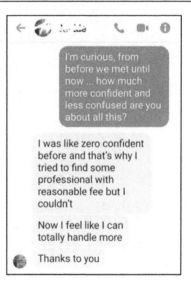

Shanda Cormier
March 4

I never had the feeling of "what am I missing" It allowed me to see the holes in the things I was not claiming, such as I did not have any records for vehicle mileage and receipts.

When you enroll in the HomeBusinessTaxSecrets.com course you also receive 'Private One-on-One Coaching' with me, allowing you to get all of your questions answered in a timely fashion, shortening your learning curve and help you to confidently fast track and convert your everyday expenses into cash through savings on your annual income tax returns. With what you discover inside the course, you may want to file amendments to past tax years tax returns and recover some home-based tax write-offs that you have missed claiming in past years.

Take the HomeBusnessTaxSecrets.com right now! Be sure to use this coupon code for a special discount: **BOOK-USD** (or use **BOOK-CAD** for Canada).

ABOUT THE AUTHOR

Doug Collins started his first home-based business in 1998 and began to discover all the ways to legally pay less income tax. While continuing to build his own home-based business in the network marketing profession since 2008, it became even more apparent to Doug how great the need was for home-based entrepreneurs to have access to a clear, understandable guideline for creating and claiming tax write-offs.

Doug found himself coaching other home-based business owners across the USA and Canada showing them how to find more tax write-offs and pay less income tax.

For Doug, this was the impetus that began the journey and the creation of the HomeBusinessTaxSecrets.com online course, which first became available in January 2019. Now, you can find Doug often on Zoom calls offering one-on-one and group coaching support. One meeting with Doug can reveal thousands in tax savings people never knew they could claim with a home-based business.

Using his 24 years experience in the corporate world combined with two decades in home-based business, Doug developed the unique ability to simplify complex ideas and create action steps to allow anyone to immediately apply strategies to build a business from home and capture more tax write-offs.

Doug also enjoys giving back as a volunteer in his community as a registered Tax Preparer with the Community Volunteer Income Tax Program (CVITP) through Revenue Canada. During the 2019 tax season, Doug completed hundreds of personal tax returns as a volunteer.

Volunteering in the community as a tax preparer has added to Doug's profound perspective on the taxation system, the impact it has on families, and why everyone should consider having a home-based business.

Doug would love to hear your stories on how this book has impacted your home-based business. Would you take just one minute and leave a sentence to two reviewing this book online? Your review can help others choose what they will read next. It would be greatly appreciated by many fellow readers.

With this in mind, Doug started a Facebook group where he has a community of like-minded readers looking to question standard advice and strive for best practice in their home-based business. The group name?

Home Business Tax Secrets

Join Doug and many others there. The moto is this: Dig deep. Find the truth. Question and share best practice – and celebrate the victories of tax savings! Want to be part of that? Join the Facebook group! Doug looks forward to meeting you.

MASTERING YOUR TAX WRITE-OFFS!

Home Business
Taxes Made Simple

Everything you need, including 'Private One-on-One Coaching'!

HomeBusinessTaxSecrets.com

Use coupon code: **BOOK-USD** (or **BOOK-CAD** in Canada)

HOME-BASED BUSINESS
INCOME TAX SAVINGS ESTIMATOR

DOWNLOAD THE MOBILE APP
www.DougCollinsOnline.com/freeapp

Made in the USA
Las Vegas, NV
21 February 2021